T0209037

One Hundred Parenting Tips

Inspired by the

Pandemic

Karen K.C. Gibson

BALBOA.PRESS
A DIVISION OF HAY HOUSE

Balboa Press books may be ordered through booksellers or by contacting:

Balboa Press
A Division of Hay House
1663 Liberty Drive
Bloomington, IN 47403
www.balboapress.com
844-682-1282

Because of the dynamic nature of the Internet, any web addresses or links contained in this book may have changed since publication and may no longer be valid. The views expressed in this work are solely those of the author and do not necessarily reflect the views of the publisher, and the publisher hereby disclaims any responsibility for them.

The author of this book does not dispense medical advice or prescribe the use of any technique as a form of treatment for physical, emotional, or medical problems without the advice of a physician, either directly or indirectly. The intent of the author is only to offer information of a general nature to help you in your quest for emotional and spiritual well-being. In the event you use any of the information in this book for yourself, which is your constitutional right, the author and the publisher assume no responsibility for your actions.

Any people depicted in stock imagery provided by Getty Images are models, and such images are being used for illustrative purposes only. Certain stock imagery © Getty Images.

Print information available on the last page.

ISBN: 978-1-9822-6405-5 (sc)
ISBN: 978-1-9822-6406-2 (hc)
ISBN: 978-1-9822-6407-9 (e)

Library of Congress Control Number: 2021903371

Balboa Press rev. date: 02/18/2021

To my daughters, Sabrina and Chelsea, who blessed me with the privilege of parenting. They continue to inspire me to pursue my mission to help other parents navigate the challenging journey of raising children peacefully instead of apprehensively.

To my husband for allowing me to experience the kind of patience, encouragement, and unconditional love I've always dreamed of finding.

To my recently-created mom support group, especially Teri Luna, Katz Yoro, and Deslynn Jaquias. Their loyalty, support, and unconditional love provided me with courage whenever I questioned my value as a parent coach.

To my daddy, who is no longer with me physically, but whose spirit always guides me to believe that my dreams will materialize as long as I persevere. To my mommy, who suffers from dementia, but whose unforgettable lessons taught me that anything is possible with faith.

To my soul sisters, Betty Charles, Jhacell Kayce, Lisa Nakasone, and Yoli Marie Gonzales. I appreciate their confidence and support during my journey as an author, parent coach, and educator.

To all the parents who struggle with distance learning challenges which add to the overwhelming stress in juggling working remotely and parenting. As a private tutor for more than twenty-one years, I received endless questions from my students' parents ranging from "How do I handle my child arguing with me over homework?" to "How can I get my children to share their worries with me?" During the distance learning phase, beginning in March 2020, I started offering virtual tutoring sessions. During July, I decided to record daily parenting tip videos until the first day of school. I posted these tips on my "Mama's Gotta Let Go" private Facebook group (since changed to "Karen Gibson: A Mom Supporting Moms" public page) as well as my public page: "Karen K. C. Gibson." I also created my YouTube channel: "Letting Go with Aloha." In addition, I conducted weekly interviews of parents, grandparents, and professionals who worked with children sharing their personal experiences and tips to help other parents who experience similar challenges as we attempt to raise responsible, resilient, and respectful children. My weekly Facebook Lives, focusing on various parenting struggles, help me fulfill my mission: to help struggling parents in the new normal guide their kids peacefully instead of apprehensively.

I had planned to record daily tips for a few weeks before the first day of school to help parents prepare for distance learning challenges. My goal changed to posting daily parenting tip videos for one hundred consecutive days. I received questions from parents about conquering distance learning challenges and found that many parents were struggling with significant stress, sleepless nights, and often frustrating arguments with their obstinate children.

This book is a compilation of the one hundred parenting tips I recorded to help decrease parenting stress and increase peace in the challenging journey of raising children.

Contents

Parenting Tip 1

EMBRACE THE POWER OF LEARNING PODS.

. . . .

Create learning pods by recruiting an adult (a grandma, an aunt, other parents, older siblings, friends, etc.) to form a study group of three to five students in a Zoom session. Every adult spends thirty minutes per week engaging students with an interactive lesson. They could read a funny story and facilitate a discussion. Children can ask to watch a short YouTube video and discuss why they liked it. A mini cooking lesson would inspire kids to share their ideas on recipes they would like to learn. A creative drawing activity could be assigned where children could share their masterpieces using crayons, pencils, or whatever supplies they have at home.

Another option for learning pods is to hire a private tutor and share the cost. I offer group rates for hourly or ninety-minute sessions. When a few parents split the cost, it becomes an affordable virtual educational opportunity.

Parenting Tip 2

INCORPORATE DIGITAL RECESS
DURING DISTANCE LEARNING.

Set your alarm to schedule specific times where kids will have recess and lunch breaks. Many kids struggle with technical challenges and questions regarding assignments. Take time to have your child go outside, eat snacks, and enjoy downtime after their distance learning sessions. Scheduling mini breaks during homework time can reduce stress and give their tired eyes and overwhelmed brains a much-needed break.

Video chatting with friends and sending funny GIFs via texting are fun ways to spend downtime. Invest in a small trampoline or a jump rope and get your kids involved in physical exercise. Playing tag, doing sit-ups, jumping jacks, or dancing to TikTok or YouTube videos are entertaining opportunities to destress through physical movement.

Minecraft, Fortnight, and other video games are popular digital recess activities that most kids enjoy after distance learning work hours.

Make sure kids know their digital recess schedule. Display it on a whiteboard or a family planner on the fridge so they know when to look forward to their breaks.

Boredom from sitting in front of their laptop or iPad can cause kids to detest school more than usual. They are imprisoned in their homes, physically away from their classmates, and they often feel confused about doing their assignments. Taking a fifteen-minute walk around the neighborhood can do wonders for their mindsets.

Parenting Tip 3

USE TIME BLOCKS TO PROMOTE PRODUCTIVITY.

Create time blocks to help organize your daily distance learning days! Teach your kids about your designated "office hours" to keep your sanity and manage your day. Kids need to know the importance of planning specific times when they are focused on their assignments. Break up their projects into manageable tasks to avoid rushing to meet the deadline the day the project is due. Teach kids the importance of having all their materials (calculator for older kids, notes, pencils, erasers, a notebook, the instructions for the project, etc.) and delegate a specific place for their supplies to avoid losing any items.

Be consistent regarding homework time frames. Electronic devices (Xbox, phones, etc.) should not be accessible, and kids must learn how to practice discipline instead of giving in to distractions. Draft and print a sheet that specifies:

- homework start and finish times
- place
- when and how long breaks are

Reassure kids that you will offer help during your assigned office hours. Parents who do not have jobs outside of the home still need office hours so they can be productive.

Parenting Tip 4

ENCOURAGE YOUR CHILD TO CREATE
THEIR OWN LESSON PLANS.

The more you allow your children to participate in their learning process, the more they may enjoy wanting to learn. It is powerful for kids to see their ideas coming to life. Children will be more motivated to learn when they are involved in designing their learning as much as possible.

Use this opportunity where many kids aren't attending a physical school to create personalized learning experiences. Choose a family project that they can manage. Create a small aquarium, plant a garden, bake a new dessert, or build a Lego masterpiece. When children feel empowered in the learning process, they will focus on and enjoy their educational experience outside of the traditional school environment.

Parenting Tip 5

MAKE DAILY READING A FAMILY PRIORITY.

Teach children to appreciate reading for pleasure and not just for academic reasons. Books provide an opportunity to travel to new worlds. The Magic Tree House series was my oldest daughter's favorite. The love of reading is often underrated, but reading can reduce stress, increase vocabulary and comprehension skills, improve brain connectivity, fight depression, and empower you to empathize with others. Reading aloud to your kids creates strong parent-child bonds, improves language and listening skills, and builds stronger emotional connections to their loved ones while they gain a lifelong love of reading.

Parenting Tip 6

TEACH THE IMPORTANCE OF MAP SKILLS AND GEOGRAPHY.

National Geographic's website[1] "deepens and gives a more understanding of history and is linked to success in math and science." Young students enhance their language skills as they collaborate and communicate about spatial relationships. Map skills include more than finding countries, states, oceans, and mountains. Kids will benefit from learning basic symbols before going outside. You need to teach map skills in stages. To avoid overwhelming them, don't do it all at once s because they won't learn as well. Plan an area for their first map-reading navigation and only teach the symbols relevant for that walk. Turn map skills into a family project where kids can draw a map of your neighborhood (make it a small area) with a legend. Use symbols, colors, or lines to represent essential places or landmarks in your community: schools, supermarkets, fast-food restaurants, and parks.

---

[1] www.nationalgeographic.com.

Parenting Tip 7

DEFINE YOUR ROLE AS A PARENT—NOT AN
EDUCATOR—IN DISTANCE LEARNING.

Your role as a parent is to motivate and encourage your child in the distance learning journey. Praise your child's successes instead of criticizing their academic weaknesses. Your role is not to be their teacher. You should guide them and teach them how to find resources to help them with their homework challenges.

Sitting next to your child during distance learning creates stress. Patience is required, which often seems impossible when teachers, students, and parents feel overwhelmed. Parents are struggling to balance their work and take care of their families. Distance learning can be challenging. As a parent, your priority is your relationship with your child. It shouldn't be about academic goals and grades. Your primary function is to support your child and help set the stage for their success. Communicate with your child's teachers and their school's administration. Release the need to control your child's academic responsibilities. It's a challenging journey that none of us expected, and many of us were not given the necessary tools to successfully play our roles.

CREATE CONSISTENT OFFICE HOURS.

To prevent constant interruptions, create consistent time frames for your kids to know when you're available for help regarding their homework, projects, and other schoolwork. Overwhelming them can prevent you from focusing on completing your deadlines and tasks because your kids might end up bothering you with their constant questions, comments, and conversations. Juggling Zoom meetings, household chores, and errands can make your day feel impossible.

Ideally, your office hours should be when you and your kids aren't too tired. Try to commit to a specific time frame for each child. Teach them to prepare their questions and have the necessary materials when they see you. Having a whiteboard or a planner on the fridge that kids can refer to—and perhaps having their names written next to their scheduled times—will prevent multiple kids from coming to you simultaneously. For example, if your son sees his brother's name planned for 3:00 p.m., he'll know that he can request his office hours with you at 3:30. Knowing the time frames for activities and tasks will make your day flow easier since your kids will see that you aren't available during "your" time.

Parenting Tip 9

CREATE A SAFE ENVIRONMENT TO EXPRESS EMOTIONS.

Many kids feel afraid or worried about expressing their feelings, especially when they feel anger or anxiety. If your child fears being judged or lectured, they might be reluctant to share their feelings and problems. Many children will internalize their worries, suffer from sleepless nights, endure knots in their tummies, and even have a hard time focusing in school.

Help children label their feelings. Describing their feelings (use a feeling wheel: jealousy, anger, sadness, fear, worry, disgust, shock, bored, hurt, embarrassed, etc.) without judgment. Once children understand that it is perfectly normal to experience negative feelings, they will be more accepting and willing to process their emotions. When kids learn that it is safe to share their feelings, they will develop empathy and become supportive adults.

Knowing it's safe to express their feelings without fear helps kids perform better in school (fewer worries) and engage in healthy relationships. Pay attention to cues your kids give—and be cautious when asking questions that may cause discomfort. Statements like: "You seem sad today" may prompt your child to open up with answers like: "Yeah, someone was mean to me" or "I failed a test today." Your role as a parent is to listen and empathize rather than give advice. Many children crave the attention of feeling heard, and empathy is a gift they will treasure.

As parents, we don't want to convey the idea that we are annoyed when they share their negative feelings. Avoid phrases like "Stop that whining, there's always something wrong with you" or "Don't you dare lose your temper with me." These phrases lead to your child forming a belief that they are not worthy of your attention. Low self-esteem and a whole set of problems can result in possible mental health issues if children do not feel worthy.

9

Keeping Your emotions in check
CRANKY
ANGRY
LOST IT
BORED
COOL

Parenting Tip 10

LISTEN AND EMPATHIZE WHEN YOUR CHILD SHARES THEIR THOUGHTS.

I asked my eighteen-year-old daughter recently what teens want from their parents, and her answer was quite simplistic: "Mom, we just want to be heard and understood. We don't need life advice. No teen wants lectures or motivational talks." Empathy and acceptance without judgment are all that teens crave from their parents.

Children are more willing to share their feelings if they aren't being judged or criticized by their parents. Validate your child's difficult emotions by asking, "Are you feeling worried about tomorrow's quiz?" or "Are you scared of that big dog walking toward us?" Stronger emotional connections are built when kids feel their parents demonstrate empathy.

Take the time to model empathy. Any time you want to teach a skill to a child, it's important to model it yourself. Many children may not understand how to practice empathy. Define the importance of kindness. It takes maturity to be aware of, understand, and be sensitive to feelings, thoughts, and experiences. It is challenging to accept beliefs that we disagree with and express a supportive response to someone who shares an opinion we feel is wrong.

Discuss emotions. Talk openly about feelings rather than dismissing or burying them. Learning to be vulnerable, authentic, and accepting others who disagree with us is a skill that promotes emotional maturity. Road rage, physical violence, and verbal abuse wouldn't be as widespread in our society if more people practiced empathy.

Parenting Tip 11

IDENTIFY YOUR CHILD'S PRIMARY LEARNING STYLE.

Is your child a visual, auditory, or kinesthetic learner? I encourage all of my students to assess their preferred learning style by using certain websites.[2]

By knowing your child's learning style, you can choose effective study methods that complement strengths rather than working against them. Some children are hands-on learners, and others work best through language and reading. Some children understand concepts better, but they might not do well on tests due to high anxiety. The secret is to find study tips that are geared to their primary learning style.

If your child practices multiple learning styles, advantages include faster comprehension and an improvement in long-term memory. Instead of just using visual methods (reading and seeing), auditory (listening and speaking), or kinesthetic (hands-on approach), the child utilizes a combination of spatial, oral, audio, and gestures. The key is to find a learning style that makes learning fun, engaging, and educational.

---

[2] I use https://cf.ltkcdn.net/kids/files/3923-Kids-Learning-Style-Survey.pdf and http://www.educationplanner.org/students/self-assessments/learning-styles-quiz.shtml.

Parenting Tip 12

Deep breathing and meditating help the brain centers for emotions and executive functioning. Children who regulate their emotions better experience fewer meltdowns. They're able to control their impulsivity while improving their concentration and focus. Many kids will complain and resist when asked to meditate. Fun ways to meditate include using the candle gazing technique. Practice this fun focusing exercise by having your child stare at a candle's flame. This simple exercise can help children improve their attention and memorization skills—and they get to blow out the candle after their meditation session.

Conscious and meditative breathing gives kids mental clarity and helps them be more present in their environment. The following suggestions may help children destress.

1. Suggest that your child close their eyes and imagine a balloon inside their tummy.
2. Have them fill up their balloon through their nose for five counts. You can ask them to make circular arm movements that signify the balloon filling with air.
3. Once they have breathed in deeply, have them hold their breath for three counts and then slowly release the air through their nose. You can make hissing sounds as the air releases from their balloon to help them visualize the activity even better.

Walk around the neighborhood, practicing being silent and just noticing the details of their surroundings. Ask your child to describe their observations. Are they aware of nature's various colors? What do they hear? How does the sun or wind feel? Noticing their surroundings helps kids focus on the present.

Illustrated by Maile Fuchshuber

Parenting Tip 13

UNDERSTAND MASLOW'S HIERARCHY.

1. Physiological needs involve giving kids the biological requirements for survival (food, clothing, shelter, etc.).
2. Safety needs involve security, feeling safe—physically and emotionally—and the need to have shelter and stability in one's life.
3. Belonging and loving others, feeling that you belong, and feeling connected, loved, and included provide much-needed comfort.
4. Esteem concerns the inner self. A sense of achievement, being recognized, having power over one's life, and feeling different from others helps a child feel valued.
5. Self-actualization has to do with achieving one's full potential, being creative, and finding that specialness of oneself.

Maslow's theory states that a positive human condition depends on a healthy body and mind. You have to attend to your children's basic needs before you can expect them to reach their full potential. If a child is suffering from low self-esteem or struggling with being bullied or criticized at home for bringing home low grades, he or she may not function in a healthy mental state. Make a cognitive assessment and talk with your child about Maslow's hierarchy. You may discover the basis of why your child doesn't feel motivated to carry out their academic responsibilities.

Parenting Tip 14

DEAL WITH ATTITUDES IN A CONSTRUCTIVE WAY.

The most frustrating challenge parents face involves oppositional, defiant attitudes. The terrible twos turn into the tumultuous teens, which sometimes evolve into the occasional resentful adult children. It's crucial to identify emotions. Start with saying, "It's OK to tell me how you feel, but you need to speak respectfully. Even if you're tired or upset, try to stay calm." Take the time to identify possible influences. What is causing your child's misbehavior? Is it the frustration of losing a video game? Perhaps it is homework stress?

Target more than the behavior—and look deeper to see what's causing the trouble. Your child may need help in learning how to handle their emotions in a healthier, more appropriate way. Challenging attitudes can help improve your child's mood. Offer words of support—and remind your children that they possess the strength to overcome a particular challenge. Support provides just the right amount of fuel to propel them to adjust their attitudes.

Parenting Tip 15

TEACH THEM PUBLIC SPEAKING SKILLS.

Children gain confidence when they practice speaking in public. Whether it's placing an order at Starbucks, going on a job interview, or presenting a speech in class, teaching your child to practice their speaking skills is a top priority to prepare for adulthood. Communication is necessary in order to express our thoughts and engage in conversations. It allows us to form connections, influence decisions, and motivate change. While some kids naturally take to it, others tend to be more fearful of standing and talking in front of a crowd. Death and public speaking are two of the top fears of most people. Give your child opportunities to practice speaking with their doctors, to waiters taking their orders, and chatting with family or friends. Encourage confidence, praise them for their efforts without criticism, and make time to record them so they can see what they sound like and look like when they're speaking.

Parenting Tip 16

LEARN YOUR CHILD'S LOVE LANGUAGE.

The best way to ensure your kids feel heard is to take the love language quiz so you can communicate using their love language.[3] Dr. Gary Chapman describes the five love languages: words of affirmation, acts of service, receiving gifts, quality time, and physical touch. Dr. Chapman believes kids need to receive love in all five love languages. However, knowing your child's top choice can help strengthen your bond and prevent behavioral issues. Identify your children's primary love language by paying attention to how they show you love.

Does your child prefer hugs over a little toy (physical touch)? Do their eyes light up when you praise them for doing a fantastic job (words of affirmation)? Some kids love to help their moms cook or want to help their dad work on his car (acts of service). My youngest daughter would scream with joy if I brought home a Happy Meal (receiving gifts). My eldest would enjoy coming into my room and sharing her favorite part of her day or any current worries (quality time).

---

[3] https://www.5lovelanguages.com/quizzes/.

I know you love me when...
Cookies just for you!
You do thoughtful things for me!
You spend time with me!
You hold my hand!
You give me gifts!
You tell me you love me!
Love Languages

Parenting Tip 17

LET GO OF PARENTING EXPECTATIONS.

Surrendering is one of the most challenging tips for parents to practice. Most parents focus on their children's future success and their perfect behavior, which may not resemble their reality. These idealized images can affect and damage how we look at our kids. Believing that our children should live up to our expectations can result in major disappointment. These idealized thoughts and feelings don't allow us to fully live in the present and be grateful for the way our children are—and not the way we want them to be.

Life becomes more comfortable when you let go of your fantasy and accept reality. Letting go of this fantasy does not happen overnight. It is a process that takes time. When parents let go of their unrealistic, fantasized expectations, they will see their children empathizing with them. Make the time to observe who they are and understand their likes and dislikes instead of demanding them to be what we feel they must be to meet our expectations.

Parenting Tip 18

TEACH YOUR CHILD SELF-WORTH.

One of the essential foundations for your child's happiness and success is self-worth. Teach them how to be self-confident by trusting their abilities, qualities, and judgments. It's also important to have faith in themselves, pride, and self-respect. When kids suffer from low self-esteem, they often have difficulty asking for help or believe they are incapable of being responsible. Some give up or may not even attempt to try. Kids who suffer from low self-esteem find it challenging to cope with mistakes, losses, and failures.

Besides loving your child unconditionally, teach your child to love themselves as they are. Teach them to see their innate gifts. Self-love is a powerful gift we can give our kids. Children who feel they do not measure up to their parents' expectations feel undeserving and may feel like the glass is half empty.

Parenting Tip 19

As an only child, I was used to enjoying my own company. I didn't realize until I became an adult how many of my peers do not feel comfortable being by themselves. They feared being without company and never learned the value of solitude. Limit your child's solitary screen time. Children of all ages will benefit from knowing how to enjoy their own company without the constant need for stimulation from others. Many parents believe that they should continuously engage with their children, but that mentality leaves no time for relaxation. Create opportunities for fun solo time. Give them watercolors, cardboard boxes, or drawing paper and send them outside to explore the backyard. These solitary activities help foster the skills children need to be successful and fulfilled: creativity, critical thinking, and confidence.

Parenting Tip 20

CHOOSE YOUR BATTLES.

Make each moment a teachable one instead of immediately resorting to punishment. Make time to validate your child's emotions without lecturing or giving life lessons. Aren't you tired of feeling like the bad parent who is constantly nagging and yelling? When you choose your battles, allow your kids to win sometimes.

Imagine being in your child's shoes. Sometimes it must feel like living with a drill sergeant who is always barking orders and harsh criticisms. When children hear no or are told to stop doing things multiple times a day, they can quickly get frustrated, leading to more power struggles. When we learn to let go and say yes, the frustrations start to dissolve.

Sean Covey's 7 Habits of Happy Kids

Parenting Tip 21

SEAN COVEY'S HABIT 1: BE RESPONSIBLE FOR
YOUR MOODS, ACTIONS, AND ATTITUDES.

Be proactive by being responsible, taking the initiative, and not blaming others for your wrong actions. Give your kids an opportunity to practice problem-solving and ask them questions when they feel powerless. Discourage self-pity by having them think outside themselves.

When children are taught to be accountable, they are less likely to allow their emotions to escalate. Understanding how feelings work helps children understand that intense feelings do not justify disrespecting someone.

Parenting Tip 22

SEAN COVEY'S HABIT 2: HAVE
A PLAN AND SET GOALS.

Do things that have purpose and practice traits that demonstrate good citizenship. Incorporate fun activities into your child's daily routine to teach important lessons about organizational skills. Introduce checklists. A simple list could be "Three things to do before bed" or "What I need to have for my distance learning classes." Invest in a fun, kid-friendly planner. Children who use planners consider their time valuable and believe completing tasks is worth celebrating. Give them fun stickers to decorate and colored pens to mark off completed tasks. Their daily tasks could include brushing their teeth (morning and night), making their bed, eating meals, and doing chores.

Work together to create family goals and personal goals. Ask your child to come up with a plan to achieve a significant dream. Include fun goals like reaching a certain level in their video games along with academic goals or extracurricular goals (creating a garden or getting a fishbowl with their favorite fish). Explain how plans need to be SMART: specific, measurable, attainable, relevant, and timely. Set clear deadlines and break their goals into specific steps that are realistic for them to achieve.

Teach Children
How To Plan

TO DO LIST

Karen Salmon
Nov 3, 2020

Parenting Tip 23

SEAN COVEY'S HABIT 3: WORK FIRST—AND THEN PLAY.

Make a plan, set priorities, and follow your schedule. Teach kids discipline in carrying out their tasks and saying "no" to activities that are time wasters. Teach them how to create a list of homework assignments for the day—and ask them to plan a schedule for how much time to allocate for each assignment. Write the estimated time frame next to each task and then write the actual time it took to complete. Kids who learn how to prioritize their work—math first, reading second, social studies third—learn how to organize at an early age.

Being accountable for what is on their priority list will make kids feel productive and proud. They can reward themselves with playtime after they carry out their responsibilities. Natural consequences can teach kids valuable lessons. They will experience less productivity when giving in to the temptation to play before completing their tasks.

Parenting Tip 24

SEAN COVEY'S HABIT 4: TEACH KIDS
THE CONCEPT OF WIN-WIN.

. . . .

Teach children that balancing the courage for getting what they want with consideration of what others want will bring them positive results. When faced with conflicts, guide them to discover peaceful resolutions rather than arguing or getting into physical altercations. Model this behavior for them when they see you experiencing disagreements.

One of the most important lessons parents want their kids to learn is how to be happy, productive citizens who work well with others. Children need to understand themselves, find their place in society, and develop the ability to understand and work with others. Children benefit from learning about character strengths. Integrity, love for learning, compassion, humility, self-care, perseverance, punctuality, patience, accountability, and self-control are examples of quality character traits.

Parenting Tip 25

SEAN COVEY'S HABIT 5: TEACH KIDS THE
VALUE OF LISTENING BEFORE TALKING.

Teach kids to respect others' views that are different from their mindsets. Do they listen without interrupting and remain confident about expressing their ideas? Do they look people in the eyes when having a conversation?

When you need your children's attention, make sure you get their undivided attention, which means making eye contact. Eliminate the word "don't" from your vocabulary. Children of all ages—toddler through teens—have a hardwired need for power. When kids hear "don't," they feel that they are losing their power. When children don't have opportunities to exert their control in positive ways—choosing what clothes to wear, helping to create the dinner menu, or picking what games to play—they tend to exercise their power negatively. Not listening is the most common frustration of parents. When you model listening, refrain from lectures and practice more silence as you allow your children to express their thoughts even when you disagree with them.

SEAN COVEY'S HABIT 6: TEACH KIDS TO VALUE OTHER PEOPLE'S STRENGTHS.

Understanding the concept of "together is better" teaches kids to get along with others, including peers who are different. Practicing being humble and seeing teamwork as an opportunity to create solutions together is a skill that will help them when they have to work with others.

The first step is to value what your kids say, which will empower them to feel that their words are worth sharing. Feeling heard and validated is the key in teaching kids to acknowledge others even when they listen to opposing opinions. Accepting others who might be different is challenging. Some children may feel intimidated by their peers or even jealous. Learning how to value their peers' strengths instead of seeing certain strengths as a weakness they don't possess helps children be open-minded.

Parenting Tip 27

SEAN COVEY'S HABIT 7: PRACTICE
BALANCING WITH EATING RIGHT, EXERCISING,
AND GETTING ENOUGH SLEEP.

Spend quality family time with family and friends. Teach kids the importance of learning beyond the classroom. Learning to reach out and help others will be a valued asset throughout their lives. The best way to model leading a balanced life is to make it a family habit to choose healthier food. Children can exercise as a family by going to the beach and racing along the shore or running around the neighborhood park. Walking around the mall is a fun way to exercise as long as you practice discipline when it comes to shopping.

Parents must train children to get adequate sleep. Lack of sleep can cause moodiness, a loss of motivation, and lower immunity. Sleep helps our bodies be fit and ready for the next day. Getting adequate rest may also help prevent excess weight gain, heart disease, and other illnesses.

Parenting Tip 28

RELEASE THE NEED TO CONTROL
YOUR CHILD'S JOURNEY.

. . . .

Letting go of expectations is one of the most demanding challenges a parent will face. When our child doesn't meet our expectations, we often are disappointed, depressed, or angry. We feel like failures. We believe that not living up to our expectations says something about us as parents. We must change our mindset and practice flexibility.

EMBRACE YOUR MISTAKES AND SHOW YOUR KIDS
HOW TO TREAT THEMSELVES WITH KINDNESS.

Children shouldn't fear failure. It is essential to let kids learn from their mistakes. When children can struggle and sometimes fail, you allow them to develop critical social and emotional skills. Don't risk their safety or not respond when they need your support. However, a parent's role is to support and guide, rather than doing the actual work. During hardships, kids can develop coping and resilience skills. Coping skills are like muscles. We don't know how strong our muscles are until we need to use them.

Illustrated by Gil Tibayan

Parenting Tip 30

ASK YOUR CHILD QUESTIONS TO HELP
THEIR DISTANCE LEARNING.

Instead of nagging kids about whether they completed their homework or why they failed an exam, let your child be accountable. Have a list of these questions next to their study area so they can review them without you nagging them:

- What classes do you have today?
- Did you write down your due dates?
- Is your laptop charged?
- Do you have supplies nearby (pencils, paper, erasers, calculator, etc.)?
- Have you emailed your teachers with any questions?
- Do you need any support from mom or dad?

After classes are over, bond with your child by expressing genuine interest without sounding like you're being bossy:

- How were your classes today?
- Did you learn anything interesting?

The objective of asking your child questions is to show them you care. You are there to guide them—not be their teacher—and be a support system.

Parenting Tip 31

TEACH YOUR KIDS THE POWER OF
POSITIVE AFFIRMATIONS.

Kids and adults have a habit of self-criticism and focusing on what goes wrong in their lives. Teaching them the importance of creating a growth mindset will train their brains to think positively. When the mind is happy, more productivity will occur—and kids will be less stressed and more motivated.

These are some powerful positive affirmations:

- I believe in myself.
- I am important.
- I am safe and secure.
- I will ask for help when I need it.
- I am amazing.
- I choose happy thoughts and ignore the negative ones.

Find an inspiring YouTube video and teach your child to play it when they first wake up or when they are about to go to sleep instead of checking social media. Your success or failure in anything depends on your mental programming, what you accept from others, and self-talk. Negative talk often leads to anxiety and depression. Teaching children the importance of positive dialogue and a healthy mindset can determine happiness or pessimism about life.

Parenting Tip 32

RELEASE GUILT AND REALIZE THE POWER
OF PERSONAL FORGIVENESS.

Carrying around guilt can lead to years of misery. Forgive yourself for your past mistakes. We often wish we could take back the mean words and actions that can lead to years of regret. No one can redo the past. Forgiveness is vital to the healing process. It gives you a chance to release anger, guilt, shame, and any other feeling you may be experiencing and move on. Once you identify what you're feeling, give it a voice—and accept that mistakes are inevitable. Don't define your current value based on your past regrets.

Parenting Tip 33

CHANGE THE GAME WITH MOTIVATION AND
GAMIFICATION DURING DISTANCE LEARNING.

Many students experience hours of boredom and lack the motivation to complete their assignments. The "gamification of education" involves increasing a learner's motivation and engagement by incorporating game design elements in the learning environment. Turning boring assignments into entertaining games can improve motivation and engagement. Game elements such as immediate positive feedback and earning badges for completing assignments are powerfully influential in increasing a student's drive to engage in these games even within the walls of a virtual classroom.

Children can earn badges for every assignment they complete. Kids are motivated by achieving levels in their video games, and the feeling of winning can be a highly motivating tool in distance learning. Ask your children what they would like to earn after achieving an academic goal. It could be something simple like getting their favorite meal or dessert when they are focused on their distance learning—and they will complete their assignments. It helps when children decide what their badge or prize will be. Set general knowledge and academic goals and create a list of various rewards when celebrating success.

Parenting Tip 34

VISIT SADNESS TEMPORARILY.

See sadness as a challenging situation that builds resilience and an opportunity to move forward. Teach your children how to cope with sadness. Make a list of "busy brain" activities together so that when they are sad, they do not withdraw or get stuck feeling low for a lengthy period. Learning how to use the right words to tell people about their sadness helps them learn how to process negative emotions.

Building emotional intelligence in children and empowering them to deal with sadness and loss are essential. Explain how sadness is a natural emotion that we feel when we experience loss, disappointment, or grief. When children learn that it isn't healthy to push away sadness or ignore it, they will learn positive ways to heal from their despair. Sadness allows you time to figure things out, accept and process loss, and adjust to a new normal. Let sorrow be their refuge, a safe place where they sort through their feelings to talk things out with someone they trust. Sadness doesn't have to be the enemy. It is a natural emotion that needs to be understood because it is impossible to avoid.

Parenting Tip 35

PRACTICE THE POWER OF PERSONAL TIME-OUTS.

Younger children go to time-out to cool down and think about their naughty behavior. Don't underestimate the power of "parent" time-outs. Many parents forget how to shift their thoughts to their "happy place." Think of a fun place where you can imagine going to by closing your eyes. It might be a tropical beach where you sit in a comfy hammock beneath a palm tree or curled up in bed with a suspenseful novel. Other time-out options could be taking a bathroom break where you listen to a relaxing three-minute meditation video or allow your kids to have some fun educational— or noneducational—electronic game time. At the same time, you escape to your room and take a fifteen-minute power nap. Power naps lower stress, improve mood, and increase focus. Preschoolers take mandatory naps for this reason.

Other time-out activities include spontaneous car rides, which might be less stressful if your children enjoy snacks and fun car games during the ride. The quiet game—where the winner is the child who remains quiet the longest—has always been a parental favorite. The license plate game exercises brain cells where everyone thinks of a word starting with each letter in the chosen license plate. The first person begins by saying "Once upon a time ..." and completes a sentence. Then the second person adds to the story. Continue with each person until the game ends.

MAKE TIME FOR LOW-TECH ACTIVITIES TO BOND WITH YOUR CHILD.

Many parents long for a time when electronics are banned. Many parents struggle with brainstorming creative activities where kids can bond with siblings and parents. Some of these options may sound boring and outdated, but you'll be surprised at how much fun and engaging they can be:

- cooking or baking as a family
- playing board games
- family paint night (with crayons, acrylics, or water paints)
- card games, puzzle races, or treasure hunts at home
- flying kites at the park or beach
- making ice-cream sundaes with fun toppings
- creating a fun play or a fashion show or dressing up in Halloween costumes
- hosting a dance party
- playing hide-and-seek
- family homemade pizza night

Parenting Tip 37

HANDLE OPPOSITIONAL BEHAVIOR FROM
TWEENS, TEENS, AND YOUNG ADULTS.

Every parent's nightmare involves disrespectful behavior, no matter what age. Don't overreact when your child acts sassy. Don't give power to rude behavior. How should you respond to sarcasm? Focus on your child's behavior and how you feel about it. Avoid any comments about your child's personality or character. Make it a priority to model respectful language. Respond to rolling eyes without losing your temper. Remain calm and choose polite words to address misbehavior. Teaching kids how to deal with anger and frustration in a socially appropriate manner will help prevent emotional explosions. It's not easy because parents are human. We get stressed, tired, and hungry. When we're in a negative mindset, our teens may push our buttons. Give yourself permission to say, "We both need a time-out to cool down before we say things we may regret later." Don't take things personally. This is challenging, but don't take what your child is saying or doing personally. Avoid power struggles at all costs. Heated situations can escalate quickly if a parent doesn't take control.

ASK YOURSELF QUESTIONS BEFORE INTERACTING WITH YOUR KIDS.

Pausing and reflecting before having a conversation with your child can prevent arguments and miscommunication. How are you processing your feelings? Are you feeling resentful? Unappreciated? Furious? Are you reacting to behavior that you're taking personally? Children ask questions at surprising times. No one can plan every conversation. However, an open mindset will allow your children to learn from their experiences. If anything, you can buy some time by saying, "I need some time before I can answer that question. Let's talk about it in an hour or tomorrow" (give a specific time frame).

Parenting Tip 39

CHANGE YOUR FINANCIAL MINDSET.

. . . .

Every time you spend money, send out a little blessing—as well as some gratitude—and say, "There is always more where that came from." This mindset frees you and your kids from the worry of your money going away, and it opens the mind to ideas and ways for more money to come back into your lives. My daughter recently shared how her belief about money was influenced by witnessing her dad and I arguing over money. Finances are one of the most common argument topics. Sex is first, money is second, and kids are third.

Children who hear arguments about a lack of money, financial worries, or judging how they waste money become adults who worry about money. We raise children with a mentality of focusing on lack. They often feel guilty spending money and believe there will always be a shortage of cash. Financial literacy is essential. Learning how to save, keeping a budget, and spending within one's means is important. Living with the fear of never having enough money can cause unnecessary stress and endless worries. I've learned that the more I believe in financial abundance, the more I attract it. For example, during the pandemic, my tutoring business tripled in revenue. Years ago, when everyone was struggling, and the economy was at its worst, I tutored one thousand sessions. I realized that I possess the power to create abundance if I stop believing in lack and trust that abundance is effortlessly coming to me.

Parenting Tip 40

CREATE EFFECTIVE MULTITASKERS.

I used to believe that productive people were multitaskers. Studies now show that multitasking can damage the brain. Since the brain can primarily focus on one thing at a time, keeping track of multiple items or juggling tasks can decrease productivity. Teach your kids the importance of focusing on one assignment at a time. Multitasking leads to stress, losing objects, and difficulty learning new material. Focusing can be a challenge.

Parenting Tip 41

FOCUS ON THE RIGHT THINGS.

Eliminate time wasters and conserve energy when you focus on your priorities. Teach your kids that distractions destroy productivity. Plan, schedule, and prioritize tasks. When it comes to homework, if a list and schedule aren't written down and followed, distractions will continuously pop up—and kids will not complete their assignments. Missed deadlines and the guilt of giving in to distractions will consume their energy.

PRAISE YOUR KIDS FOR THEIR HARD WORK
INSTEAD OF LABELING THEM AS "SMART."

Praising a smart son or daughter for their intelligence may make them feel anxious and unprepared to deal with failure. "It is much better to praise a child for effort," Claudia Mueller and Carol Dweck, researchers at Columbia University, advised. Child development experts have been warning parents that telling kids they're smart causes them to fear doing anything that might disprove this praise. Children may avoid pushing themselves and making mistakes.

Refrain from saying, "You're so smart!" Instead, praise your child by saying, "Look at what a great job you did!"

Parenting Tip 43

ACCEPT NO SHAME FOR ASKING FOR HELP.

Many children feel they are incompetent if they ask for help. Some feel their peers will judge them if they raise their hands in class or ask for clarification if they don't understand the material. Parents can remind kids not to be embarrassed about asking for help. The hardest part is teaching kids not to care what others think. Fear of judgment may result in adults who crave praise to boost their self-esteem.

Parenting Tip 44

ENCOURAGE YOUR KIDS TO THINK CRITICALLY.

Many children are impatient and want answers *now*. No one likes to feel frustrated or incompetent. To raise independent learners who don't give up when the journey gets bumpy, kids need to experience problem-solving by themselves.

Provide children with opportunities to have fun. Offer opportunities to practice critical thinking. Pause and wait. Resist the temptation to rescue your child because you see tears or frustration. Kids will learn to trust themselves to solve their problems without running to someone for help if they are given opportunities to practice logic, reasoning, and hypothesis testing. Asking "what if" questions will provide them with opportunities to predict possible outcomes. Ask what they think might be a possible solution, reassuring them that it's OK if they're wrong. Their brain cells are practicing hypothesizing, which can lead to independent thinking skills.

Parenting Tip 45

FAILURE IS THE MOST CRITICAL INGREDIENT IN SUCCESS.

. . . .

No parent enjoys watching their child fail. Their failure becomes our failure. We want to prevent their heartbreak, frustration, depression, or disappointment. However, to build resilience, they need to fail so they can pave the road to success.

The worst decision a parent can make is to prevent their child from failing. When children are protected from failing, they often feel powerless and have no control over their own journey. They also may become dependent on others to rescue them.

TEACH YOUR KIDS NOT TO WORRY.

Children can benefit from relying on faith and releasing worry. If worrying becomes a lifelong habit, something as small as a nagging concern in the back of your mind can affect your heart. It can make you more likely to have high blood pressure, a heart attack, or a stroke. When kids see their parents worrying, they learn that worrying is a part of life. Some kids believe that worrying means they are caring. If they didn't worry, it would mean they didn't care.

Making worry lists and talking through each worry can help children release stress about negative scenarios. Practice thinking strategies so they feel prepared to handle challenging situations. They will learn that they are strong enough to tackle any obstacles that come their way. Kids who learn the power of faith become adults who don't spend sleepless nights overcome with endless worries.

TEACH YOUR CHILD PERSEVERANCE.

Kids who are encouraged to persevere live with gratitude, receive praise, set reasonable expectations, and don't allow obstacles to steal their joy. Parents offer support when problems arise, but they don't fix their children's challenges. When their children make mistakes that lead to negative consequences, they refrain from saying, "That's why you should never ..." or "You should have planned better or known better," which can haunt kids throughout their adult lives.

Parenting Tip 48

UTILIZE CONVERSATION STARTERS.

Conversation starters can help parents build emotional connections with their kids. Kids who feel accepted are less likely to lie. If they feel respected and are given time to listen and be heard—and not be scolded or lectured—they grow into adults with higher self-esteem and are happier overall. Some questions parents can ask include:

- What were the worst and best parts of your day?
- What would be your favorite superpower?
- If you could go anywhere, where would you go?
- What's the silliest face you can make?
- Are you worried about an upcoming event?
- If you could be any animal, what would you be? Why?
- How do you think your friends handle peer pressure?

Parenting Tip 49

It is natural for parents to continually worry about their children's futures. Stop wasting your energy worrying about what lies ahead for your child. Instead, concentrate on what's happening with them right now. Focus on their strengths and the happy memories that warm your soul. The worst thing we can do as parents is take away our children's sense of accomplishment. When we try to figure things out for them, we are stealing the opportunity for them to experience life's challenges. The key to stopping the fears and worries about how they will turn out if they do not become responsible, resilient, and responsible is letting go of feeling responsible for their actions.

You can only guide them, be a positive role model, love them unconditionally, and let them soar on their own. Put things in perspective. Many situations are way worse than your child's current challenge. Imagine the worst—and then realize it's unlikely to come true. The fear in our heads is always worse than reality.

Parenting Tip 50

CHALLENGE BORED KIDS.

Bored kids are looking for challenges. Your attempt to fix their boredom will just bring frustration for you and them. Instead of giving them options for entertaining themselves, remind yourself that there are worse things than being bored. Your responsibility is not to cure their boredom. Vent to someone—not to your child—to release your frustration.

You could empathize by saying, "So, you're bored, huh? Nothing to do?" Then, listen. Some kids just want your attention. Give them eye contact, sit closer to them, and make them feel like they are essential. Listening opens up communication channels. You may not have ideas that interest them, but giving them your attention and quality time can be a magical solution.

Parenting Tip 51

The main tip for raising a confident child who sees their self-worth is to appreciate their efforts no matter what. Kids who feel judged by their grades or whether they met their parents' expectations can feel stressed if they don't measure up. Keeping your disappointment to yourself is crucial for building a child's self-esteem.

Encourage your child's curiosity and offer them challenges that test their patience. When they overcome obstacles, offering them consistent praise will show them you acknowledge their perseverance and accomplishments. If they fall short of their goals, be sure to reassure them that their results do not define their value. Grades, awards, and achievements should never be how they determine their success.

Parenting Tip 52

AVOID YELLING AT YOUR KIDS.

Yelling, criticizing, and lecturing damage a child's self-esteem. Yelling often involves harsh insults that can be qualified as emotional abuse, which is known to have long-term effects, including anxiety, low self-esteem, and increased aggression. Criticizing your kids and screaming at them can change the way their brains develop because humans process negative information and events more quickly and thoroughly than good ones. The next time you are frustrated and tempted to yell, pause and take a deep breath. Will yelling help your child behave? Will they be open to your advice?

Parenting Tip 53

TEACH YOUR CHILDREN NOT TO BELIEVE EVERY
THOUGHT THAT ENTERS THEIR MINDS.

It's normal for us to believe every thought that pops up in our heads. Neuroscientist and philosopher Dr. Deepak Chopra shared that we have an average of sixty thousand to eighty thousand thoughts per day. According to the National Science Foundation, about 80 percent are negative thoughts, and 95 percent are repetitive. If we repeat those negative thoughts, we think negatively more often than we think positively. Teach your children to see their thoughts as separate bubbles that they have control over. They can visualize popping every negative thought bubble that appears in their minds. They can surround themselves with optimistic people to train their brains only to choose to believe uplifting thoughts.

Parenting Tip 54

TEACH YOUR CHILDREN NOT TO HOST A PITY PARTY.

Releasing the chains of victimhood isn't easy. It's easy to blame others for your circumstances. Do you hear your kids blaming you for being at fault for them losing their concentration during an important video game? Some kids will say, "It's all your fault. I never get to ..." How can you teach your child to be a victor and not a victim? The first step is to have them recognize self-loathing and blaming others for their situations. Possessing a victim mentality is addicting and more comfortable to deal with than facing challenges. Next, they must recognize when they view past events with regret instead of as learning opportunities. Last, comparing their achievements with their peers often leads to hosting a pity party. When children don't feel good enough, it's an instinct to feel sorry for themselves.

DON'T DENY YOUR CHILDREN'S DREAMS.

Some parents say "Get your head out of the clouds," "You will never make money playing video games," "Choose a career that will give you financial stability," or "You know how unrealistic it is to dream of becoming an actress or a singer?" These comments will rip apart a child's self-esteem. Many parents—often out of desperation to increase the chance for their children's success—make choices that leave their kids with low self-esteem. What should parents say when a child wants to be a ballerina photographer who plays the violin as her career? That was my youngest daughter's dream in middle school. I've learned to say, "Wow! Wouldn't that be fun?" Don't make judgments. A child's dreams will evolve, and sometimes they change weekly. The key is to support and nurture your child's passions so they learn to believe in the wondrous possibilities that lay ahead. Their dreams may be silly and unrealistic in your eyes, but don't burst their bubble when all they desire is your support and approval.

Parenting Tip 56

TEACH YOUR CHILDREN THAT POWER
NAPS HELP THEIR BRAINS.

Research shows that you can make yourself more alert, reduce stress, and improve cognitive functioning with a nap. The length of your rest and the type of sleep you get can determine the brain-boosting benefits. A twenty-minute power nap can be good for alertness and motor skills—and even typing or playing the piano.

Adults who nap ten to twenty minutes per day feel more refreshed and recharged.[4] The next time you find yourself unable to focus and feeling drained, treat yourself to a power nap instead of resorting to a caffeinated beverage.

---

[4] www.healthline.com.

PRACTICE THE ART OF BEING INTERESTED.

Most children's deepest desire is to gain their parents' undivided attention. How many times do parents hear, "Listen," "Watch me," or "Wanna see this funny TikTok?" Practice engaging with your children, letting them know that their interests are vital to you. Support them in their hobbies. When Pokemon Go was popular, I remember seeing parents take their kids to wherever they wanted to go to capture the most wanted Pokemon of the day.

My girls loved it when I would go ice-skating with them since they enjoyed taking ice-skating lessons and wanted me to skate by their side. Respond with sincere interest when you're busy and your child says, "Do you know what I did today?" or "Want to watch what my favorite YouTuber posted today?" Watch their smile broaden—and witness the emotional connection.

Parenting Tip 58

CREATE A CONSISTENT BEDTIME ROUTINE.

Many kids dread going to bed. It means the end of their day, the end of playing, and the end of having fun. Creating a consistent bedtime routine will end the struggles of forcing kids to go to sleep. Set a schedule where your kids know they have to start preparing for bedtime. Sharing or reading a story, talking about their day, brushing their teeth, putting on their pajamas, removing electronics from their room, and wishing them "sweet dreams" creates a comforting scheduled routine. Kids who know what to expect are more likely to cooperate because they feel secure knowing their daily schedule. They are less likely to disobey when they know what to expect every day.

Parenting Tip 59

Apologizing requires a lot of courage and vulnerability. The magical healing power of saying "I'm sorry" can heal years of damage in a relationship. I never witnessed my parents apologizing to one another. Why is apologizing so hard to do? Saying sorry often means that you're at fault. But what are you conveying? Does your child understand *what* they are sorry for? Do they understand how their words or actions caused someone physical or emotional pain?

Make it a priority to have a conversation discussing what happened, why it was hurtful to the person they're apologizing to, how they can address the hurt they caused, and what they can do to change their behavior. If the apologies are said reluctantly, these words do nothing to address the behavior; instead, they remain the standard apology that children continue to use into adulthood. For the apology to heal both parties—since the person causing the hurt sometimes feels guilty—the apology must be felt, heard, and accepted. Teaching the proper way to apologize is vital for children. The person apologizing must admit that they did or said something that caused someone emotional or physical pain. Admitting mistakes can be challenging to own.

Parenting Tip 60

THE WAY YOU PARENT AFFECTS YOUR CHILD'S FUTURE
SUCCESS, HAPPINESS, AND MENTAL HEALTH.

Your parenting style, words, and actions affect your child's belief system, self-esteem, and values. Many studies have shown that parents who have a negative approach will raise children who have a higher susceptibility to depression. Negative parenting actions that lead to depression include low emotional and physical support, physical punishment, and an unhealthy expression of negative emotions.

Negative approaches include criticizing, expressing negative emotions regarding children's behavior, and not allowing children to express themselves, which may lead to children who grow up suffering from self-esteem issues. If children don't feel supported or accepted precisely the way they are, they may grow up to suffer in dysfunctional relationships.

Parenting Tip 61

TEACH YOUR CHILD THE JOY OF
GIVING OR VOLUNTEERING.

. . . .

Volunteering fosters empathy and a sense of self-efficacy, provides experience working with other people, and helps children develop new skills. Communities benefit from children giving their time, energy, and skills to help those who are less fortunate. Kids who give back to their communities stop focusing on their interests and see how they can make a difference by helping others who are suffering and in need of their volunteering efforts.

Teach children the importance of investing in their communities. We want our kids to be successful in their work and personal lives and to learn what it means to be a responsible and compassionate citizen.

Parenting Tip 62

HELP YOUR CHILD LEARN THE IMPORTANCE
OF SETTING BOUNDARIES.

Children who do not learn how to set boundaries often grow into adults who allow others to take advantage of them. Healthy personal boundaries are essential for healthy relationships, and parents should begin teaching their children about boundaries from a young age. Help your kids build confidence in their emotional health. Learning how to maintain healthy boundaries will build strength and teach children how to grow into independent adults who respect their own decisions without needing to please others. Teach your children to tell their friends when they are not happy with their friends' behavior. Confident children will be comfortable being assertive and are not afraid to stand up for themselves. They can say, "I don't like it when you ..." or "It's my turn now."

Parenting Tip 63

TEACH YOUR CHILD HOW BIG AND DIVERSE
THE WORLD IS BY BEING OPEN-MINDED.

Learning about diversity teaches children to respect and celebrate the differences in all people. It also creates more tolerant adults who aren't afraid to explore. Learning about different cultural aspects offers new experiences for children. Show children that diversity is a strength. Build their cultural identity and boost their self-esteem by giving them chances to share their strengths. Emphasize how scary it can be to feel like you are different from other people and how brave it is to share unique things about yourself or your family. To reduce biases and support your child's development of compassion and understanding, explicitly tackle stereotypes and prejudices.

Parenting Tip 64

TEACH YOUR CHILD THE POWER OF PATIENCE.

Children find it difficult to understand the need for patience. The concept of time is not yet entirely developed—and neither is their sense of delayed gratification.

When you set a time frame for something (you'll get a snack when you arrive at your destination, etc.), they're going to ask if it's time yet frequently. Stay patient, kind, and positive when questioned—even if it's for the twentieth time. Your children are not trying to be selfish or mean-spirited in their questions; they simply can't conceptualize time yet. Scolding them for asking too many times will reinforce the idea that waiting is a negative experience. However, staying calm and positive while they wait reinforces that waiting can be a positive experience. Practice deep breathing exercises and understanding that patience builds resilience. Kids who don't learn the power of patience may want to escape hardships and expect that their desires happen immediately.

TEACH YOUR CHILD THE POWER OF
POSITIVE QUITTING: QUITTING THINGS
THAT NO LONGER SERVE THEM.

As our children grow, they will quit jobs, places, and relationships; if they didn't, we'd have great cause to worry. Not all of their decisions will please us or prove to be good ones, but nobody lives a perfect life. So, while our children are young, isn't it wise to offer them some guidance in quitting?

Teach children to quit things that aren't working for them. When they stop tolerating all the negative things that hold them back, they'll make room in their life for more positive experiences. Quit unhealthy habits, end unhealthy relationships, and say no to people who are taking advantage of you. Can you imagine how happy we would be if we stopped procrastinating, stopped worrying about things that are out of our control, and stopped doing things that aren't beneficial to us?

Parenting Tip 66

OFFER YOUR CHILD OPTIONS RATHER THAN
DICTATING WHAT THEY MUST DO.

Parents in previous generations used to raise children with one central theme in mind: obedience. It didn't matter how you felt, what you thought, or what you wanted. As a child, your parents trained you to do as they demanded. Emotional development and self-expression in children give them an important voice. We should ask, "What are we doing with that voice now?"

Parenting is entering a new generation where emotions are dictating our every move. Children whose parents put their feelings first are navigating the world through a happiness lens, and if they are not happy, they are likely not engaging. The process of life becomes looking outward versus inward, and children may become experts at finding other people's flaws. In that process, they lose the ability to process their own flaws. It is *their* journey—not *your* journey.

Parenting Tip 67

Kids and preteens typically worry about things like grades, tests, their changing bodies, fitting in with friends, the goal they missed in the soccer game, or whether they'll make the team. They may feel stressed over social troubles like cliques or peer pressure or feel bullied or left out. Currently, kids are worried about the pandemic, whether distance learning will ever end, and if life will ever return to the way it used to be.

As parents, we can help our kids handle worrying by being available and finding out what's on their minds. Encourage kids to put what's bothering them into words, ask for key details, and listen. Sometimes just sharing the story with you can help lighten the load. Show you care and understand. Don't minimize their worries. Worrying about whether they will make it onto the soccer team is equivalent to an adult worrying about whether they will be able to pay their mortgage. Show compassion and guide them toward brainstorming solutions (without fixing their problems). Teaching kids to keep problems in perspective can lessen their worries and build strength, resilience, and the optimism to try again. Remind your kids that whatever happens, things will be OK.

Parenting Tip 68

TEACH YOUR CHILD THE IMPORTANCE
OF PRACTICING FLEXIBILITY.

Learning how to go with the flow and stopping rigid mindsets requires teaching cognitive flexibility. Kids will benefit from learning flexible thinking as well as *set shifting*, which is the ability to let go of old ways of doing things and trying new ways. Kids who can think about problems in new ways engage in *flexible thinking*, and kids who get stuck in their patterns tend to engage in rigid thinking.

When kids engage in flexible thinking, they can better cope with change and new information in the classroom—and out in the real world. Kids with weak, flexible thinking skills struggle to take on new tasks and have difficulty solving problems. They can become frustrated when life doesn't go their way, which can lead to increased stress in relationships and at work.

Parenting Tip 69

TEACH YOUR CHILD TO MAKE
DECISIONS WITHOUT REGRET.

A new study from Ireland's Queen's University looked at the role of regret involving kids' decision-making skills and found that children go on to make better decisions after experiencing regret. It can be painful to realize that a different decision would have led to a more positive outcome. However, as parents, we need to allow our kids to experience regret and learn the natural consequences of their choices. They will have the opportunity to gain valuable life lessons. The best action a parent can take is to guide their children while allowing them to make choices that may result in regret. See regret as a stepping-stone to building resilience and learning what not to do the next time a similar situation arises.

Parenting Tip 70

TEACH YOUR CHILD HOW TO OVERCOME HARDSHIPS.

The best way to train your children to handle challenges that feel like you're allowing your child to navigate life in dangerous waters without a life preserver is to let them figure things out independently. Do not come to their rescue or give in to their tears and emotional pain. It's challenging for a parent to witness a child suffering, but if we don't allow our kids to fail and experience hardship, they will not have the opportunity to resolve problems independently or find the right resources without leaning on their parents for help.

Play problem-solving games as a family. Teach your kids that making mistakes provides the best opportunities for gaining wisdom. Showing your children that you trust in their abilities to face fear instills self-confidence in them.

Parenting Tip 71

MAKE SELF-CARE A PRIORITY.

As an educator for more than twenty-five years, I've realized that many parents fear experiencing mental breakdowns. If parents do not make self-care a priority, sanity is often hard to keep. Self-care can be something as simple as watching a thirty-minute comedy or engaging in an activity that fuels your soul. Take a fifteen-minute walk around the neighborhood or soak in a relaxing bubble bath for twenty minutes. If parents don't ask for help, sanity may be difficult to keep. Parenting doesn't have to be solitary. Venting and sharing your worries with a friend can relieve some of the stress. Managing everything from household chores, tending to work responsibilities, helping children with their distance learning, motivating them, and enforcing discipline can be overwhelming. Life can feel like juggling a dozen razor blades.

Parents can help prevent parental burnout by delegating tasks that can be done by others. Find another family member to take care of time-consuming tasks like laundry, grocery shopping, and preparing meals. Keeping one's sanity is often the primary goal of most parents.

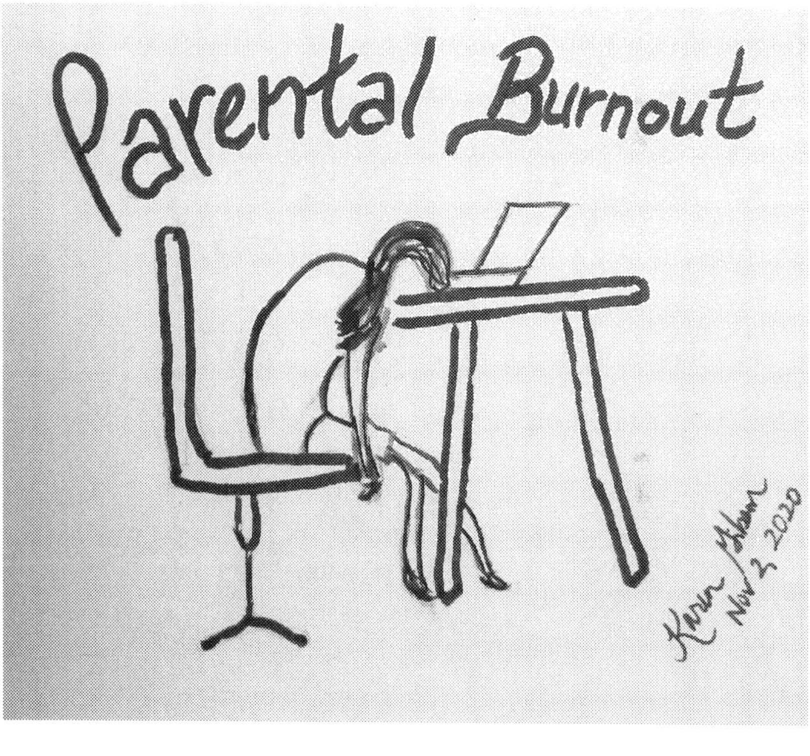
Parental Burnout
Karen Gibson
Nov 2 2020

TEACH YOUR CHILD HOW TO HANDLE DISTRACTIONS.

Many parents don't teach their children to remain focused by training their brains to handle distractions. Digital distractions, wandering minds, and allowing their attention to focus on the "next interesting thought" can steal their focus. Many parents do not empower their kids with the autonomy to control their own time.

Allowing kids to be responsible for how they use their time is a tremendous gift; even if they fail from time to time, failure is part of the learning process. Parents need to understand that it's *OK* to put their kids in charge because it's how they learn to practice monitoring their behavior.

Many parents don't trust their kids to make the best use of their time and end up micromanaging them, shouting reminders of what they should be doing, and losing their tempers when their kids' attention wanders. We must learn to let our kids lose track of time and suffer the consequences of being distracted. We can also teach them how to be mindful and monitor their behaviors. When kids learn how to manage their own time and behaviors, they often grow up to be adults who successfully conquer distractions.

Parenting Tip 73

DO NOT ALLOW YOUR CHILD'S RESPONSIBILITIES
TO BECOME YOUR RESPONSIBILITIES.

· ·

Being responsible is essential for a child's success in school and in the real world. How can parents stop worrying and trust their kids to be responsible? Allowing a child to do it *their* way will encourage a feeling of pride in accomplishment and foster a sense of responsibility.

Considering the shift from obedience to responsibility raises the question of how involved parents should be in helping their children. Not wanting your children to fail can lead to doing too much. If that happens, the children won't learn how to take on the responsibility themselves. On the other hand, there are times when children need guidance, support, and information to learn how to be responsible. Find a balance between overmanaging and under-parenting. Communicate unconditional love when administering discipline, setting boundaries, and giving guidance.

Parenting Tip 74

CHANGE YOUR CHILD'S BAD MOOD BY MAKING THEM FEEL LOVED!

Discovering your child's love language is the key to making a child feel loved. If your child is in a bad mood, it's a sign they are not feeling heard, understood, or unconditionally loved. Have your family—parents and kids—take a quiz to discover how the child feels loved.[5] Do they crave quality time? Words of affirmation? Physical touch? Gifts? Acts of service?

When you love children by utilizing their primary love language, that lousy mood will melt away. You'll experience more peace and less conflict in your household.

---

[5] https://www.5lovelanguages.com/quizzes.

Parenting Tip 75

TEACH YOUR CHILD HOW TO ORGANIZE,
PLAN, AND KEEP A TO-DO LIST.

Organizing and planning are learned skills. Getting organized can make life easier for kids with learning and thinking differences. It might take some effort in the beginning, but it's worth it in the long run.

Teach kids how to break tasks into chunks and use a planner and checklist for their daily to-do lists. Teach them the importance of time management. If kids learn how to block out time for specific tasks and schedule downtime, they will have a system in place as an adult to practice organizing their personal and professional lives. Distractions and procrastination still exist, but having a schedule to rely on will help keep them on track.

Parenting Tip 76

TEACH YOUR CHILD TO SET GOALS.

Setting and writing down goals and making dreams are so important. Practice being. According to a parenting tool, GoalUP, which was created to help parents motivate their children, every goal should be specific, measurable, attainable, relevant, and time bound (SMART). It is vital to have children practice thinking of a specific goal they would like to reach and go through the steps needed to achieve their goal.

Use a chart and action steps they need to take so they can measure progress and stay focused. Setting measurable goals and celebrating when those goals are reached can pave the way toward a successful and happy adulthood. It provides an opportunity to experience setbacks and not allow disappointments to stop taking action steps.

HANDLE CONFLICTS WITHOUT EMOTIONAL OUTBURSTS.

Conflicts and emotional outbursts are a part of the parenting journey. Teaching children how to identify their feelings is a great start. Once they identify their feelings (anger, jealousy, sadness, confusion, etc.), they can start pinpointing their triggers. What caused them to feel that particular emotion?

When emotions are still intense, it's not the right time to problem. Instead, solve the conflict itself. Help kids come up with coping skills to use if they need to calm down in the middle of a meltdown. This might involve splashing cold water on their face, taking some deep breaths, or playing with a pet. A positive distraction can make a huge difference in handling conflict with a healthier mindset.

Parenting Tip 78

Children who look for happiness externally (through physical things, situations, etc.) will always be chasing happiness. Teaching children the importance of self-love encourages them to value their strengths and trust that happiness resides internally. Self-love is demonstrated by making your child feel important. Listen to what they say, make eye contact with them, and allow them to express themselves without judgment.

Teaching your children to express themselves and love themselves unconditionally takes time and effort, but it's one of the most important things you can do for them. All of us have experienced moments when we felt like our parents weren't listening to us. We felt like they didn't understand what we were going through or didn't have time for us. It happens to everyone at least a few times, but ongoing failure to meet a child's emotional needs can cause a lifetime of struggle.

Parenting Tip 79

Help your children safely express their anger.

Carl Rogers, an American psychologist and the founder of the humanistic approach to psychology, said, "The truth about rage is that it only dissolves when it is really heard and understood, without reservation." Children who are not taught how to safely express their anger often have tantrums, screaming fits, or difficulty remaining calm.

When parents accept and empathize with the children's emotions, they learn that emotions aren't dangerous. They understand that they do not have to act out their anger. As we accept our children's anger and remain calm, they learn the emotional skills to calm themselves and communicate how they feel without hurting people or property.

Parenting Tip 80

ESTABLISH THE CORE FAMILY VALUES OF
RESILIENCE, RESPECT, AND RESPONSIBILITY.

In order to raise children who are resilient, respectful, and responsible, teach them moral values like honesty, loyalty, respect, self-reliance, self-discipline, patience, kindness, gratitude, forgiveness, personal responsibility, and courtesy. These values help in developing a strong personality for children, which minimizes the possibility of making poor choices.

Modeling your family's core values teaches children how to practice being responsible and respectful. Resilience is taught by allowing children to experience challenges in life independently—without relying on their parents to save them from making mistakes that will teach them lifelong lessons. If a child forgets to complete a project a few hours before the due date, and a parent comes to the rescue, the child will not learn how to be accountable when deadlines are missed.

Parenting Tip 81

TEACH YOUR CHILD HOW TO ACCEPT UNCERTAINTY.

. . . .

Whether it's a canceled family outing, a fallen ice cream cone, a scoreless soccer game, or a broken promise due to unforeseen circumstances, life is full of disappointments. While the gut instinct of the caring parent might be to sweep the disappointment out of the way by offering a quick solution, parents can't always protect their kids from letdowns.

During the insanity of Covid-19, the closure of schools, and the awkward transition to distance learning, children experience a lot of unpredictability and disappointment. Children are worried about when they will finally return to school without wearing a mask and washing their hands frequently. Empathize with your child. Kids all process things differently. Some may resort to anger, others may be scared, and others might not know how to react. The three questions to ask are:

1. How did you feel when it happened?
2. What do you wish had happened?
3. What could be done differently?

If there is no control over the situation, like in the case of a global pandemic, encourage conversations about how they can feel safe. Wearing masks and not being able to attend large group outings is temporary. Taking the time to have a conversation with your child offers comfort during unpredictable situations and can be an opportunity to bond.

REMAIN LEVELHEADED WHEN YOU FEEL LIKE YOU'RE ABOUT TO LOSE IT.

All parents experience moments where a tornado of emotions tears through their homes. Validate everyone's feelings and avoid shouting mean words that can cause mental and emotional damage. Your role is to be a thermostat that monitors your own temperature, your children's temperatures, and even the temperature of your spouse or significant other.

Children act out when they don't feel validated. They feel life is unfair and want you to know it by engaging in an emotional explosion. When you feel like you're about to lose it, tell your children in a calm voice that you need a personal time-out. Take several deep breaths, splash some cold water on your face, inhale peppermint oil, or call a friend to help you reclaim your peace. When you do lose your temper, take the time to apologize to your child and explain why you engaged in an emotional explosion. Be a positive role model by saying sorry whenever you make a parenting error, and they will learn the importance of apologies.

Parenting Tip 83

DEFINE CLEAR CONSEQUENCES FOR YOUR CHILD.

Children respect and follow the rules better when boundaries are set and consequences are defined. Consequences are not meant to make your child feel humiliated, embarrassed, or unloved, but they should make your child realize that certain behaviors will not be tolerated. If your kids respect you, consequences will be much more effective. At a minimum, plan to give your children fifteen minutes of positive—undivided—attention each day.

Consequences should have specific times. "You're grounded until I say so" or "You can't leave the house until I can trust you" are vague consequences. Giving consequences without a specific end time may be a sign that you're not really serious and that you may be making an empty threat in the heat of the moment.

Parenting Tip 84

Parenting is a job that is a lifetime commitment. Daily challenges can cause us to feel like frustrated failures, but simple daily actions can make parenting less stressful. It is best to be aware of the big picture to keep you from losing your sanity. Not reacting and taking the time to take deep breaths without losing your cool will save you from suffering sleepless nights or days of regrets.

Self-care must be a priority for every parent. If we function on an empty tank, tempers will flare, which can result in rebellious kids who are also tired and feeling like their emotional tanks are depleted as well.

Parenting Tip 85

DISCUSS THE UNCOMFORTABLE TOPICS WITH
YOUR TEEN: SEX, DRUGS, AND ALCOHOL.

Conversation starters in a safe environment can provide a nurturing space to motivate your child to be open to discussing uncomfortable topics. Questions with a nonjudgmental tone can spark meaningful dialogue.

- Why do you think teens drink alcohol and do drugs?
- Have you been in situations where there were opportunities for drug or alcohol use? Did you feel pressured? Why or why not?
- Imagine that it's twenty-five years from now, and you have a son or daughter who is the same age as you are now, what would you say to them about drinking and drugs?

Sex is a taboo topic that many teens refuse to discuss with their parents. We want kids to think critically about sex rather than just acting emotionally and impulsively. Ask them what they think the benefits are to being sexually active as a teenager? Research finds that one-quarter of young women regret losing their virginity to the "wrong" partner and that one-fifth have significant regrets about having unprotected sex or progressing too quickly sexually in a relationship. Ask them what they think about those statistics. Ask them if they believe there are good reasons or bad reasons for becoming sexually active? The "sex talk" is no longer about the mechanics since kids learn about this emotionally charged subject at a younger age. The talk may include some uncomfortable questions, and if it's too much for a parent, find an aunt, uncle, or trusted adult family friend who your child is comfortable with.

Parenting Tip 86

DON'T LET ANGER CONTROL YOUR MIND.

One of the ways to keep your sanity when you feel like you're about to lose it with your child is by taking several deep breaths during emotional conflicts. When you allow your anger to get the best of you, it affects the immune system, heart, brain, blood pressure, and even digestive system.

According to Harvard-trained and published neuroanatomist Dr. Jill Bolte Taylor, anger actually lasts for ninety seconds:

> To feel an emotion, we need to think a thought, which then stimulates an emotional circuit in our brain, which in turn creates a physiological response in our bodies. Within ninety seconds from the initial trigger, the chemical component of your anger has completely dissipated from your blood, and the automatic response is over. If, however, you remain angry after those ninety seconds have passed, then it is because you have chosen to let that circuit continue to run.

All emotions last for less than ninety seconds. It is a choice to hang on to the anger and allow it to control us. Walk away, blast your favorite song, eat your favorite snack, or take a ten-minute shower while deep breathing and visiting your happy place. The key is to "go brain-dead" by not allowing anger to control your mind.

Parenting Tip 87

EMPOWER YOURSELF WITH PATIENCE.

If parents don't practice patience, there will be more conflicts because their moods will be dictated by their children's behaviors. Identify the trigger points that cause your anger to escalate. Patience means remaining calm—even in the face of a child's extreme acting out. We all have limits to how much we can tolerate. This doesn't make us *bad* parents; it makes us *normal* parents. Be a positive role model of how patience is practiced. Show your family how to practice patience when they need to wait in long lines, are stuck in traffic, or are frustrated when the Wi-Fi doesn't work.

You've just survived a stressful day working and are preparing dinner, refereeing an argument between two of your kids, and helping another with his homework. Your daughter asks you— for the umpteenth time—for something you've already said no to, causing you to yell, "No!" It shakes the entire house. You ask your son to pick up his dirty dishes—also for the umpteenth time—and find yourself using a tone of voice that belies any sense of calm or composure. Never underestimate the power of deep breathing. Whenever you feel that patience is a virtue you don't have time to practice, take a deep breath and be aware of your thoughts. Remind yourself that you don't have to allow impatience to control your actions.

Parenting Tip 88

DO NOT CLIP YOUR CHILD'S WINGS.

Helicopter parents hover overhead by constantly overseeing every aspect of their children's lives. These parents strictly supervise their children in all aspects of their lives, including social interactions. This parenting style often creates moms and dads who see their identities wrapped up in their children's accomplishments. If their children earn poor grades or make unwise decisions, they feel personally responsible.

They fear for their child's future. Lack of trust in children's decisions and believing that they require your intervention to prevent failing causes many parents to be too actively involved in their children's lives. The solution is to simply allow your child to experience failures—and the natural consequences—and figure out life. Support them when they fall, but don't clip their wings and prevent them from experiencing failure. Resilience can't be built without overcoming hardships.

HEY! Did you bring your lunch?
MOM! STOP Nagging me!
Helicopter Parenting

Parenting Tip 89

PRACTICE THE MAGICAL POWER OF
PARENTAL MINI VACATIONS.

Whenever a parent has a few minutes to gain some sanity, take advantage of these moments to mentally regroup and release some stress. Dedicate ten minutes to listening to your favorite music while you're driving somewhere without your kids. When your children are engaged in playing video games or watching Disney or Netflix shows, take the time to curl up in bed and read some inspirational quotes or watch a heartwarming YouTube video that nurtures your soul.

If you take a five-minute walk outdoors, breathe some fresh air and notice nature's beauty—and you'll be amazed at how some of your stress will magically melt away. Notice birds chirping or leaves swaying on trees without a care in the world. Gain perspective on how there is so much more to life than the overwhelming stress that consumes your soul. Take time to write your accomplishments of the day in a journal. No matter how minor, doing laundry, washing dishes, taking a shower, or picking up take-out food for the family are all tasks that you completed. If you had a lazy day, use this time to write a to-do list. The simple act of writing can be calming to your mind. If you own a pet or have the opportunity to interact with one, hugging a fur baby can uplift your spirits and give you some much-needed unconditional love. These mini vacations and mini breaks can bring balance to your mental health.

Parenting Tip 90

GUIDE YOUR TEEN IN UNDERSTANDING THE
IMPORTANCE OF THEIR EMOTIONAL WELL-BEING.

· ·

If you're operating on an empty tank, your children aren't learning the importance of caring for their own emotional well-being. Experiencing major stress, choosing unhealthy eating habits, lacking quality sleep, and feeling like your world is in constant chaos are signs that your emotional tank is running on empty. Children who witness parents who do not take care of their mental health grow into adults who repeat this unhealthy pattern. Simple actions like deep breathing, meditating, drawing, dancing, and reaching out to mentors can prepare kids to strengthen their emotional intelligence—recently seen as more important than IQ—to successfully deal with overwhelming struggles.

Teaching your child coping skills for dealing with stress can minimize mental breakdowns during challenging times. By helping children learn to respond to their emotions in a constructive manner from an early age, parents empower them to navigate future emotional struggles. It may even help teens avoid depression and anxiety. The secret is to help kids put negative situations into perspective. Learning how to discover constructive solutions to problems that seem overwhelming helps support teen mental wellness.

SHOW YOUR CHILD THAT YOU LOVE THEM UNCONDITIONALLY.

Many parents don't realize the conditional love they demonstrate to their children. Speaking in a harsh tone, using a critical look when giving advice, or reminding them of forgotten tasks or mistakes they've made can cause them to feel incompetent. Many of my students feel sad when they disappoint their parents or when their actions cause extreme anger.

Expressing your unconditional love can be as simple as saying, "I love you no matter what!" If your child fails a test or falls behind on their assignments, remind them that you will never judge them based on their grades. Hearing "I still love you even when you fail a test or fall behind in school" can make the difference between a child feeling loved and supported and feeling like a rejected outcast.

I ♡ U even if...

FEARS
MELTDOWNS
OUTBURSTS
Why did you do that?!
I WILL ALWAYS LOVE YOU
RAGE
TANTRUMS

I ♡ U no matter what!

Karen Gibson

Parenting Tip 92

USE THE NINETY-SECOND RULE TO HANDLE ANGER.

This parenting tip sounds like a repeat of "how to avoid losing your sanity" and "how to keep your cool," but I feel like it's necessary to explain how the ninety-second rule works. Self-control is always available if you practice the ninety-second rule. Brain scientist Jill Bolte Taylor, the author of *My Stroke of Insight*, described our ability to regulate the ninety-second rule:

> When a person has a reaction to something in their environment, there's a ninety-second chemical process that happens; any remaining emotional response is just the person choosing to stay in that emotional loop.

This is a powerful discovery. This means that you have ninety seconds to decide whether you want to allow your anger to control you and stay in that emotional loop. When someone pushes our buttons, it's because we don't possess the impulse control or we're not aware of another way to respond to the upsetting situation. No situation and person can make us feel or do anything. It's truly up to us whether to carry our anger.

Chronic reactivity creates a stressful biochemical boomerang that weakens the immune system and increases the likelihood of a heart attack or stroke. So, the next time you feel immense anger, remind yourself of the severe consequences of engaging in an emotional explosion. Focus on deep breathing for ninety seconds with your eyes closed instead of giving in to your tempestuous temper.

Parenting Tip 93

PARENT FROM A PLACE OF GRATITUDE.

One of the top complaints I hear from parents is not feeling appreciated by their children. Boredom, confusion, frustration, and the constant demands of parenting create overwhelming stress. By connecting with gratitude during difficult parenting moments— rather than feeling frustrated and annoyed—a sense of calmness is possible. Rather than mentally grumbling your way through your frustration, parents will be able to appreciate their challenging situations by practicing gratitude.

When you can't imagine how you'll ever achieve peace, when you feel like pulling every strand of your hair out because of the constant sassiness your teen dishes out, or when you are so exhausted that you are tempted to resign from being a parent, choose a mindset of feeling grateful. Gratitude will be your savior in the midst of chaos. Realize that you are in a negative mindset, and like your teen, you may require an attitude adjustment. Think of three blessings in your life: your comfy bed, a safe home, and the financial means to provide food for your family. Enjoy the power of gratitude. Whenever you are facing a parental struggle, see it as an opportunity to practice being thankful.

Parenting Tip 94

APPLY A GROWTH MINDSET WHEN
DEALING WITH A FRUSTRATED CHILD.

Dealing with temper tantrums, disrespectful looks, and harsh words from your child create opportunities to apply a growth mindset. Pay attention to the words your child is saying as well as how you choose to react. When children feel like life is unfair and they are not heard or understood, they express it the only way they know how to, which is by engaging in an emotional explosion.

Teaching children how to accept that life won't always go their way will prepare them for disappointments. Explain how a fixed mindset—needing life to go their way or else—versus a growth mindset will determine if they will experience struggles that feel life-threatening when they are just facing hardships that build resilience. It's crucial for children to realize that they are not helpless. They can grow and adapt. It is a life-changing lesson to see themselves as capable of growth. However, it is also possible for someone who is challenging us to experience positive changes. This perspective releases some of the pressure kids might feel and helps them think more in terms of challenges than threats. Challenges can be overcome. Threats create a mindset of going to battle to conquer the enemy.

Parenting Tip 95

YOU CAN INCREASE YOUR CHILD'S SELF-ESTEEM.

Children who are raised with harsh criticism and who feel like they can never measure up to their parents' expectations often suffer from low self-esteem. Self-esteem is tied to how capable and valuable a child feels. Giving your child ways to recognize their strengths boosts self-esteem. Self-esteem is how much kids value themselves and how important they believe they are in their world.

Parents who allow their kids to make mistakes without judgment are more likely to become confident adults. Start by forcing yourself to stand back while your child takes healthy risks. Too many parents are constantly trying to rescue their kids from failure. Even if their choices sometimes have negative results, allow them to make their own choices—as long as their decisions don't jeopardize their safety.

Parenting Tip 96

CHANGE YOUR PERSPECTIVE OF ANGER.

No one enjoys being angry. Anger clouds your perspective. Learning how to manage your anger can prevent high blood pressure and other health risks. You can choose to manage your anger or let your anger manage you. You have choices about how you respond to the world around you. For example, when someone mistreats you, you have choices about how you perceive that person's actions.

The next time your child pushes your buttons, approach it with a sense of curiosity. Did your child bruise your ego? Did their sassy behavior cause your temper to flare? Pause, take a breath, and remind yourself that you have a choice to change your perspective. When you're in a state of rage, you become deaf, dumb, and blind to everything that's going on around you. Choose peace instead of engaging in an emotional explosion that may teach your child to follow your footsteps when they are annoyed.

Parenting Tip 97

DECLUTTERING IS IMPORTANT—
MENTALLY AND PHYSICALLY.

Keeping your mental and physical space free of clutter can be challenging. Clutter affects mood, depletes energy, and increases stress. Kids who worry about failing an exam or being bullied have mental clutter that can cause focusing problems and even depression. Learning how to process and release worries can clear mental clutter.

The National Institute of Mental Health found that kids living in a severely cluttered environment often have elevated levels of stress, experience less happiness, and have more difficulty making friends. Clutter can cause social isolation because kids will feel uncomfortable having friends come over because they will witness the clutter. Teaching kids how to be organized, toss any items that no longer serve them, and deal with mental health issues will help them handle physical and mental clutter as they grow into adults.

Parenting Tip 98

TRY WORKING WITH A PARENT COACH.

Most parents don't think twice before having their son work with a football/soccer/baseball coach. I've known single moms who hire private baseball trainers for their kindergarteners. When a student is failing, I'm hired—even when parents can't afford my hourly fee. Some parents invest in a monthly tutoring fee of $660, but many parents don't see the value of working with a parent coach.

A skilled parent coach helps moms and dads understand challenging relationships with each other and their children. They learn strategies to correct behavioral issues. Parents and children can make simple changes that serve as a foundation for stronger and healthier relationships and a better life. Parent coaching offers completely judgment-free, confidential support to help you when the stress seems unbearable. All this support can be provided in the comfort of your own home.

Parenting Tip 99

YOU CONTROL YOUR OWN EMOTIONAL LIFE.

. . . .

Parenting involves a mix of love, discipline, consulting, and guidance. Great parents show their children they are loved no matter what—even in worst-case scenarios. The most challenging part of parenting is keeping one's cool when a child disrespects you or doesn't follow instructions. How does a parent handle the frustration and disappointment if their child is arrested? What if the child swears at them in anger?

What is the secret to loving children when they give you an attitude, refuse to do homework or study for exams, experiment with alcohol before the legal drinking age, or don't obey your rules? Realize that you control your own emotional life. Are you taking on a responsibility that is not yours? Keeping this perspective in the midst of anger seems impossible. However, if you practice this one tip, you will save your sanity and help your kids grow into adults who feel unconditionally loved, accepted, and valued. It is normal to feel intense hatred toward your child when they exhibit challenging behaviors. Remind yourself that your child's value isn't defined by their poor choices or misbehavior. It can be easier to focus on the situation that is causing such extreme anger instead of on the child.

Parents may feel embarrassed, helpless, or angry, and those emotions don't lead to feelings of like or love. It's important to keep in mind that your child's behavior is their attempt to get unexpressed needs met, which does *not* reflect on your parenting. Focus on your child's strengths. Focus on loving them no matter what!

Parenting Tip 100

YOU CAN LEAVE A PRICELESS LEGACY.

. . . .

What matters more than discipline? Nurturing and cultivating your relationship with your child. Modeling how you interact with your spouse or partner. Creating fun memories, traditions, and experiences as a family. When a child doesn't feel heard, understood, and valued, the bond you have with them falls apart. They will resist discipline, they won't respect you, and they may rebel.

Be an example of the character traits you would like your child to develop. Do you want them to remember your angry outbursts years after you're in heaven? What do you want your great-great-great-grandchildren to know about you? Loving your children with commitment and unconditional love is the greatest legacy you can leave. Be honest and open by sharing childhood stories and turning conversations into priceless memories that will be treasured. Share your struggles and the demons you've encountered with your teens, and they will cherish the lessons you've learned. Let them know the real you rather than the perfectionist parent you long to be.

What Now?

I hope that some of these parenting tips resonate with you. The truth about parenting is that we all make it up as we go along the emotional roller coaster of raising children. Every parent wishes there was a manual showing the way to avoid the struggles, stress, and shame we experience. Unfortunately, it's more of a trial-and-error journey where we learn along the way.

This insane global pandemic, as well as the challenges of distance learning, inspired me to share parenting tips to guide moms and dads as they navigate the unpredictable parenting journey. I have been an educator for more than two decades. I have heard so many horror stories of parental burnout and experienced my own mental meltdowns as a mom. I've learned that complaining about parenting exacerbates the mental, physical, and emotional harm to our bodies and brains. Focusing on gratitude can change our focus from feeling frustrated to feeling thankful. On a final note, here are a few more suggestions to help ease your parenting journey:

- Release the need to control your child's behavior and decisions (unless it endangers their health).
- Practice being calmer than your child. Responding with patience is easier when you're in a calm mental state.
- Say sorry when you lose your temper or say words that hurt your child's self-esteem. Apologizing nurtures the parent-child bond, creates closeness, and leaves a treasured legacy.
- Words spoken in anger can cause lifelong wounds. Your child may react with rebellion, but every child's self-esteem is damaged when harsh criticism is yelled in the midst of conflict. Keep in mind the cliché "If you can't say something nice, don't say anything at all."

- Stop worrying about grades. Instead, guide your child toward finding their passion so they can satisfy their hidden potential for excellence and contribute to society. It's inside them—and getting straight As is unlikely to help them get it.

Enjoy the journey, accept the bumps along the way, and trust in your child's journey. When you have faith in your child, let go of control, and love unconditionally, you will be proud of the amazing adult you raised.

Please follow my YouTube channel: Letting Go with Aloha. I would love to hear from you! Email me at Karen@LettingGowithAloha.com. Find me on Instagram @lettinggowithaloha. Please request to join Karen's private Facebook group: Stressed Mom Support Group by a Hawaii Mom.

Sabrina, Karen's eldest daughter (left), Karen Gibson (middle),
and Chelsea, Karen's youngest daughter (right)

Karen with her husband Thomas

Printed in the United States
By Bookmasters